KNITTING FOR BEGINNERS

A simple guide For the realization of your masterpieces, both for children but also for adults. From the basics to start knitwear, to alternative techniques, to classic socks.

MARYANN CRAFTS

Table of Contents

Introduction.

Knitting is making fabric with yarn using two or more needles. Loops are made on one needle as the starting point and then the fabric gradually grows by drawing other loops through them as they are passed back and forth on the needles, moving from row to row. Confused? Don't worry.

Beginning knitters will look at the yarns and needles and patterns and get a little bit overwhelmed. But as if you keep at it, you will soon discover that knitting is actually very easy, and you only need to learn two stitches to make any knitted article: the knit stitch and the purl stitch. So, are you ready to get in on the fun?

The Origins of Knitting

Knitting was mainly done on silk, wool, and other fibers that decay rapidly, even in the most controlled, most perfect conditions. Knitting needles are just an ordinary pair of sharpened sticks and could have been anything, a pair of hair picks, skewers, maybe spindles, or any of the other million uses you could think of sharpened sticks; so it's really difficult to identify them as actual knitting needles beyond any reasonable doubt.

Knitted items in the past were all done by hand and yarn, a valuable item, was not disposed until it has completely worn out to the point of disintegrating. Knitted sweaters that do not fit anymore can easily be unraveled and re-knitted over and over again. Not many people had the brilliant idea to save their everyday items for their children. Leaving heirlooms was not a major consideration.

Because of these factors, no one really knows the exact origins of knitting. It's all a huge mystery; and with solid evidences missing, there are not that many valuable knitted items left for us to discover. All experts, and the rest of us, can do is make intelligent guesses derived from fragments and scraps found in museums around the world.

Linguistically speaking, knitting is a fairly fresh invention. The Oxford Unabridged English Dictionary says that the term 'to knit' which means 'to make loops with two long and straight needles' was only added to the English language in the 14th century. The term 'to knit' did not appear in any European language before the Renaissance.

While it's true that knitting has not been around for very long, and that its past is quite bunched up in knots, pun intended; one thing remains. That thing which had made knitting an instant hit when it was invented and makes it popular today is its sheer simplicity. With two sticks and a ball of yarn, you can literally make anything; sweaters, gloves, socks, scarves, bonnets and hats, bags, and so much more. Knitwear is as just as popular as ever before. Even science has jumped on the bandwagon. Engineers are now using knitting techniques for metallic shields for hoses and doctors are starting to knit nylon arteries used to transplant organs. One thing is for sure; Knitting may not have a solid past, but it has a bright future ahead of it.

The Health Benefits of Knitting

Knitting has existed for many centuries; first and foremost, as a way to survive. In its purest and earliest form, knitting sprouted from the basic human need to protect the body against heat, cold, and other elements.

Many centuries later, with the many ready to wear and cheaper, not to mention easier options; humans do not depend on making their clothes by hand. With a short trip to the mall and a flick of small plastic card, you can get any type of handmade or machine-made clothing you want.

Knitting, today, is no longer a necessity; however, over the years, it has gathered a huge following who take up the craft as a hobby. Why shouldn't they? Besides the obvious advantage of making your own useful and unique articles and garments, knitters also enjoy physical and psychological health benefits from knitting.

- Knitting helps you clear your mind by engaging your brain in a creative activity and helping you forget the stresses and anxieties you experience every day.

- The rhythmic motion you follow when knitting has been expertly proven to change the brain's movement; releasing good hormones such as serotonin and dopamine which makes you feel happy and relaxed.

- These rhythmic repetitive movements also help distract knitters from mulling over the past and pondering about the future. Knitting helps keep you in the moment. The relaxation response is not only good for your psychological well-being; it is also good for your physical health as it is known to control blood pressure, heart rate and prevent stress related sickness.

- Moving your eyes from side to side is also helpful. Therapists using Eye Movement Desensitization and Reprocessing (EMDR) have proven that moving your eyes from side to side or rolling your eyes is a potent yoga exercise and has worked wonders with trauma patients.

- The learning process involved in knitting helps you feel good about yourself and helps improve your self-esteem. Studies also show that as you learn and master more complicated stitches, you gain the confidence to try out new things in other aspects of your life.

- Through knitting, you will be accustomed to following and identifying patterns, learning new movements, using both your hands, and yes, even learning math. It helps improve fine motor skills and keeps the mind active. Knitting develops dexterity, concentration and basic arithmetic.

- Knitting, as well as other crafts, engages both body and mind. This causes optimistic feelings about life in general. As surveys have proven, knitters are inclined to be more sociable, friendly, positive, and outgoing.

Besides having a one of a kind knitted article that you invested blood, sweat and tears on, the health benefits of knitting are also outstanding. Knitting in the ancient times was a way for people to survive. Knitting now is a way for people to stay alive, happy, and healthy. Many centuries have come and gone but one thing remains; we are still knitting for our lives. Start your wonderful knitting journey today.

Chapter 1: Supplies

- Yarn

The choice of yarn and needles depends largely upon your pattern. Typically, knitting patterns suggest a yarn and may suggest a starting needle size; however, this doesn't necessarily provide you with all you need to know to successfully knit a garment, pillow or other project. You may knit tighter or looser than the original designer or you may want to use a different yarn than the one recommended. You might even want a larger or smaller finished product.

When you are knitting, the yarn and needles work together, and both are equally important to the finished look of the end garment or item. Some issues are a matter of personal preference, like bamboo or metal knitting needles. Others impact the finished size of your knitting, like the size of your needle and weight of your yarn.

- **Types of Yarn**

A visit to a yarn shop or your local craft store reveals yarn in every color, weight and fiber. Shelves, baskets and bins may overflow with yarn intended for every garment, from lace to heavy sweaters and scarves. Some projects will work with nearly any type of fiber but understanding the fundamental qualities of each fiber will help you choose yarn you enjoy working with and produce garments that are wearable and practical.

1. Animal Fibers

Yarns made from fleece, hair and fur are some of the most popular choices for knitters of all skill levels. Inexpensive wool yarn is an ideal choice for early knitting projects, because it is forgiving, easy to work with and has enough stretch to accommodate a loose or tight knitter. More expensive animal fiber yarns range from sturdy to delicate, depending on the fiber and yarn weight. Most craft stores carry at least a few wool or wool blend yarns; however, more costly animal fiber yarns are often only available at specialty shops.

2. **Wool**:

Wool comes from sheep. The sheep are sheared regularly, and the wool is washed, combed into long fibers and spun into yarn. The quality of the yarn depends upon the quality of the fleece, with different breeds producing softer or coarser fleece, and wool yarns range from quite coarse to extremely soft. While wool has a reputation for being itchy, knitters know that many types of wool feel nice against the skin. Your own sense of feel and texture is the best tool to choose a wool yarn you will enjoy wearing.

Yarns labeled farm wool, felting wool, fisherman's wool or Icelandic wool are apt to be rather rough, but extremely durable. These yarns may even retain some of the natural sheep lanolin, making them quite water resistant. While you would not choose one of these yarns to wear against your skin, they make fine outerwear, including warm cardigans. These wools are also ideal if you would like to feel, or mat, the fibers together to form an exceptionally thick and durable fabric, ideal for potholders, oven mitts and tote bags.

Many wool yarns are not super-soft but are very wearable. If your skin isn't too sensitive, these yarns work for a wide variety of applications. They can be felted, but can also make perfectly nice pullovers, scarves and hats. If you have delicate skin, you may want a camisole or tee under a sweater made from these wools. The most common wool in this category is Cascade 220 and similar yarns.

Softer wool yarns include Merino wool, which is often described as cushy or buttery. These yarns feel soft and smooth against your skin and work well for socks, pullovers and even baby items. Merino and similar wools are also ideal for gloves, fingerless mitts and scarves. Even the most delicate skin will tolerate and like these fine and soft wool yarns.

Super wash wools offer the benefits of wool, plus one. While most wool yarns require relatively delicate care, including hand washing and flat drying, super wash wools are treated to stand up to machine washing. Super wash wools, including those used for socks, can be machine-dried, but will be longer lasting if treated somewhat more gently.

3. **Alpaca**:

Like wool, alpaca is an animal fiber taken from the fleece of an alpaca, which is smaller cousin of the llama. Alpaca yarns are very soft, but can be rather delicate and fragile, depending on how they are spun. These are not the workhorse yarns that make your hard-wearing hiking sweater, but rather the fine yarns that make a delicate lace shawl for formal wear or a soft cardigan for special occasions. Alpaca-blend yarns are more versatile and durable than pure alpaca and can be used for projects that will get more wear.

Alpaca is also extraordinarily warm which makes it ideal for special hats, scarves, gloves or knitters living in very cold environments. If you live in a warmer environment, you may find alpaca knitted garments too warm for comfort.

4. **Mohair**:

   Mohair is a delicate and fuzzy fiber made from the hair of angora goats. It may be blended with sturdy wools or delicate silks. While the soft halo it creates can be pretty, some people find even the softest mohair blends itchy against their skin. Mohair blend yarns are occasionally used for sweaters but are more commonly used for shawls and scarves. Sturdy mohair and wool blends will be felt, making them a good choice for oven mitts and other felting projects.

Angora: Like mohair, angora has a fuzzy halo; however, angora is much softer than mohair. Angora comes from the coats of angora rabbits and is either sheared with clippers or gently pulled once it is loose. The removal process depends on the type of angora rabbits that are used. Angora is often associated with fitted 1950s sweaters. Angora blends are a good choice for fine, fuzzy scarves and delicate sweaters. However, angora is not suitable for hard outer wear.

5. **Cashmere**:

   Ready-to-wear cashmere sweaters are costly, as are cashmere yarns. Cashmere yarn is the spun hair of a cashmere goat. Their coats are slow-growing, and the fiber is quite costly to produce.

Cashmere is very soft and warm; however, pure cashmere is an indulgence most knitters cannot afford. Several companies produce lovely and relatively affordable cashmere blend yarns. Producers frequently mix the fine fiber with merino wool and silk. Cashmere is a lovely choice for a special project, like a soft scarf or a luxurious pair of cashmere blend socks.

6. **Silk**:

Silk yarns are made from the cocoon of the silkworm. Like silk fabrics, these yarns are typically very soft; however, some have slubs or variations in the yarn, creating a coarser texture. Unlike wool and alpaca, silk yarns are appropriate for all year-round wear and are good choices for warm-weather knitting. Yarns made of 100% silk are relatively rare, but you will find silk-blend yarns in many shops. Silk yarns and blends with a lot of silk typically drape nicely and feel good against the skin; but they can be rather slippery and hard to knit. Silk blends include wool or other animal fibers, as well as linen and cotton blends.

Uncommon Animal Fibers: There are a number of uncommon animal fiber yarns that you will occasionally see, particularly in specialty yarn shops. While alpaca yarn is common, several other animals in the same family also produce usable fiber. Llama fiber is quite soft, while camel is less so. If you are prepared to invest in a special project, vicuna yarn, made from a smaller cousin of the alpaca, is especially fine. You may find mink yarn or other yarns produced by fur-bearing animals, as well as the rarest of animal fibers, qiviut, made from the fur of the musk ox. While these yarns are typically quite nice, in many cases, you will want to save them for special and small projects due to the cost.

- **Plant-Based Yarns**

1. **Cotton**: Cotton yarns are durable and hard-working, but they have no stretch and can be tiring to knit. They are relatively unforgiving and do not block well. Mercerized cotton has a high sheen, while non-mercerized cottons have a matte finish. The most common cotton yarns are dishcloth cottons, ideal for kitchen items, but not for clothing. Better quality pima cotton or mercerized cotton can make lovely summertime garments, as can cotton-blend yarns.

Casual items, including hand knit kitchen items, can be machine washed and dried. Sweaters or shawls in softer cotton yarns can be machine or hand washed, but they will wear best and retain their color if treated gently.

2. **Bamboo**: Bamboo is a soft yarn with a great deal of drape, but very little body. It can be quite slippery to work with, but

it produces a beautiful garment, particularly when you want a very fluid garment. Bamboo may be a difficult choice for beginners, given that it has a tendency to slip and is often very difficult to rework if you make an error.

3. **Linen**: Linen yarns produce very light garments which are ideal for summer wear. Because linen yarn can be quite coarse, you can soften your finished project with washing and wearing it. Linen is frequently mixed with other fibers, including cotton, viscose and hemp. Linen yarns also make excellent face cloths or very fine lace, with crisp stitch definition. Sturdier knit linen garments and household items will stand up to machine washing and drying, while finer ones, like lace, should be handled with more care.

4. **Hemp**: Hemp and hemp blend yarns are relatively uncommon but resemble linen yarn in many ways. These yarns are rather coarse but do soften with use. Consider hemp for market bags and other non-wearable items. Like linen, hemp will soften with time, machine washing, drying and wear.

5. **Rayon and Viscose**: Rayon and viscose are both produced from cellulose or plant fiber. The fiber is heavily processed, but produces a soft, drape able yarn. Rayon and viscose are typically blended with other fibers in yarns and are especially common in novelty yarns, such as chenille and boucle. Some of these yarns are rather durable, while others are quite delicate. Check the laundering instructions on the yarn you choose; however, most of these yarns will do best if laundered by hand.

6. **Corn, Soy and Other Plant Fibers**: While cotton is the most common plant fiber, you may also find yarns made from less likely plants. There are a few companies that produce yarn from soy, corn and kelp. These yarns are quite soft, and its texture can be compared to silk. They often have a high sheen, but like other very soft yarns, they may be slippery and challenging to knit. Follow the manufacturer's recommendations for care and laundering.

- **Synthetic Yarns**

1. **Acrylic**: Acrylic is the most common synthetic fiber. Amongst knitters, you will find that acrylic often has a bad reputation, which is sometimes well-deserved. Some acrylic yarns are very inexpensive but feel rough and scratchy. Better quality acrylic yarns and acrylic-blend yarns are durable, washable and can be quite soft. These yarns are ideal for washable garments or larger items, like afghans.

2. **Nylon**: While nylon is used exclusively in some novelty yarns, it is more often added to yarn blends. Nylon can make wool yarns more durable or provide shimmer and sparkle to a traditional yarn. Since nylon is commonly blended with other fibers, the traits and characteristics of the yarn are typically determined by the base yarn.

3. **Polyester**: Like nylon, polyester is commonly blended with other fibers. Polyester is relatively versatile; however, the final structure and care of the yarn depends upon the other fibers in the yarn. Keep in mind that synthetic fabrics, like polyester, are not particularly breathable and may be hot when worn.

- **Yarn Weight**

Bulky and DK Weight Yarns: Yarn weights range from very fine laceweight, not much heavier than sewing thread, to super-bulky yarns. Very fine yarn will knit as many as 10 stitches per inch and a super-bulky yarn will knit two to three stitches per inch. Most patterns suggest a yarn or may recommend a yarn weight.

- **Sport and Worsted Weight Yarns**

Lace and Fingering Weight Yarn: The recommended yarn and needle sizes are only a suggestion or starting point. Your own knitting may require that you use a larger or smaller needle to get the appropriate size garment or item.

- **Buying Yarn**

Yarn is typically sold in a hank, skein or ball. Hanks of yarn are large loops, twisted to form a neat and sturdy bundle. Knitting directly from the hank leads to a tangled mess. Hanks should be wound into balls by hand or on a ball winder. Skeins of yarn are already wound into a workable, center-pull oval-shaped or slightly oblong ball. These can be worked as they come from the store. Balls of yarn, like skeins, typically should be worked from the center.

When working from a center-pull ball or skein, avoid using the strand of yarn coming from the outside of the skein. Reach into the center and find the loose end. Gently tug on this end and work from the center of the skein out. If you insert the skein into a disposable zip-closure bag or small container with a hole to thread the yarn through, it can reduce the risk of knots as the ball becomes smaller.

- Needles

Knitting needles come in different sizes, styles and materials. Common needle sizes range from a size 0 to size 17. Patterns will often provide you with an idea of where to start. Also be prepared to go up or down a needle size if needed.

Needles are available in wood, bamboo, plastic, acrylic, and metal. You may wish to experiment to figure out which types of needles you prefer. Bamboo or wooden needles are less slippery and may be lighter, while metal needles are often sharper and faster. These are tools and you will find you enjoy knitting more if you invest in good quality needles.

While many knitters begin with traditional straight needles, there are several other options. Traditional straight needles range from 8-inches to 14-inches in length. A plain or decorative tip keeps the stitches on the needle.

Many knitters prefer circular knitting needles over traditional straight needles. Circular needles consist of two tips, which are typically 4-6-inches in length and attached by a flexible cable. Cables range from short to quite long. These needles, commonly called circs, can be used to knit flat or in the round and are more versatile than straight needles. Any project that can be knitted on straight needles can also be worked on circulars and these can be used to work flat or in the round.

Double point knitting needles are used for knitting in the round and making I-Cord. Sold in sets of five, these are short, straight needles with both ends sharpened to a point. Beginners should feel free to choose either straight or circular needles for their first projects. Double point needles can wait until you are ready to knit socks or need to knit i-cord for the first time.

- Other Knitting tools

Accessories

There are a few basic accessories that are a useful addition to any knitting bag. They include a ruler and a knitting gauge. The knitting gauge enables you to measure your knitting and it has holes allowing you to measure and check the size of your knitting needles. Another useful addition is stitch markers, which are small plain or decorative rings that can mark off a number of stitches. As you progress, you may want to include a cloth tape measure, yarn needle and crochet hook in your knitting bag.

Picking Additional Supplies

Pick a pattern. You can find lots of cost-free knitting patterns on-line, or you can acquire knitting pattern books for every little thing from clean cloth to hats and lap coverings. Check out some designs online or in a pattern book to locate a project that you want to make.

A pattern is likewise a practical overview of the materials you will require to complete a job. Always check your design and also obtain the precise kind of yarn, needles, as well as various other products indicated for the task.

Get a set of sharp scissors. Sharp scissors are a must for knitting. You might only need to utilize them for your task, or you may find out on your own using them every 15 mins if you have to change your yarn out a lot. Keep a set helpful while you are functioning.

Buy some stitch markers. Sew pens are little plastic rings that go around your needles to mark the start of a stitch. They are especially valuable for intricate jobs and also for noting the beginning of your stitches when weaving in the round.

Try out cabling with a cable hook. Cabling daunts lots of knitters when they are doing it for the first time, yet wiring is a lot easier than it looks. A cable hook is necessary for cabling, so make sure to choose one up when you feel prepared to experiment with this technique. They are available in several dimensions.

Get some end protectors. End protectors help your weaving needles to prevent the yarn from sliding off when you are working or pausing. These are particularly valuable when you are weaving on double finished needles. However, you can position them on completions of any needle when you are prepared to put it away for the day.

Keep a tapestry needle available. You can acquire large eye plastic tapestry needles in craft shops to help with completing your knitting projects. These are crucial for weaving in the long run of your knitting task and also adding decorations like pompoms on hats.

Get yourself a cute knitting bag. You will require a huge place to maintain every one of your products, so get a weaving bag on your own. If you don't wish to buy a bag, then you can likewise assign a canvas bag or tote as your knitting supply bag.

Chapter 2: Starting Knitting.

- How to hold yarn and knitting needles cast on

How to Hold Needles and Yarn

There are different ways to hold the needles and yarn and there is no right method since it will be the one that is most comfortable for you. The yarn can be held in both the right and the left hand, the needles can be held above or below.

Try both styles, they will be uncomfortable and slow at the beginning, but you have to keep trying until you discover which weaves more simply and naturally. The best style will be the one that suits you best and with which you enjoy knitting.

Hold Needles and Yarn with English style

(The thread in the right hand):

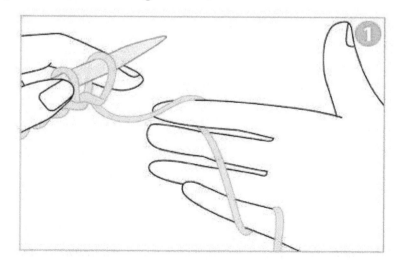

1. Begin by placing the thread in the fingers: wrap the pinky finger with the thread, then pass it under the two middle fingers and finally over the index finger of the right hand.

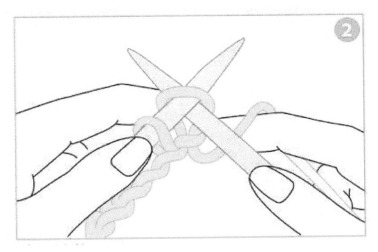

2. With the needle of the points already mounted in the left hand, grasp the empty needle with the right hand while the yarn of the ball is intertwined in the fingers to maintain tension.

Knitting with Continental Style

The Continental style also known as the German style, is the most popular weaving method in northern and Eastern Europe. When weaving with this style, the lacing of the way it is done with the English style is not performed. In this case, it is used to link the same needle and is passed through the point of the left needle. When doing this, a small movement is made with the right-hand needle. To weave with the Continental style, it is necessary that the yarn of the ball is in the left hand. Advanced weavers prefer this style since it requires a smaller number of movements per point and the right hand never has to release its needle, resulting in a faster weaving method.

Hold Needles and Yarn with Continental style

(the thread in the left hand):

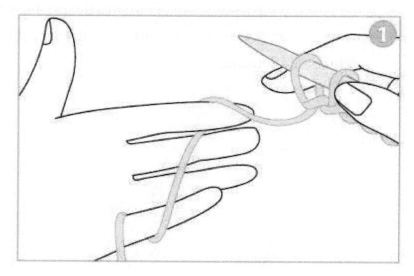

1. Begin by placing the thread in the fingers: wrap the little finger with the thread, then pass it under the middle two fingers and finally over the index finger of the left hand.

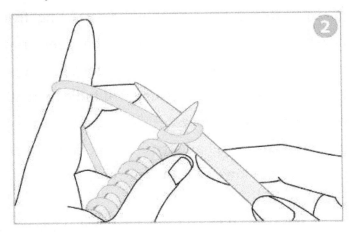

2. With the needle of the points mounted on the right hand, pass it to the left hand, while the yarn of the ball is intertwined in the fingers to maintain tension. Grasp the empty needle with your right hand. Practice these steps and you will soon weave rhythmically and evenly.

How to Pick Your Yarn

Even advanced knitters get flabbergasted with the selection of available yarn. There are just so many beautiful choices! There is always something new. You can fritter away days going through the different options, enjoying the textures and the colors. It can be overwhelming how many choices there are and a challenge picking just the right one for your project. The purpose of this is to help you gather your supplies, so here is where you will learn how to pick your yarn.

Choosing a basic, worsted wool yarn in a lighter color is excellent to learn on. Choose a medium yarn weight rather than thin or thick. Make sure the texture is smooth. This will be the easiest to learn and practice on. When purchasing from a commercial yarn or craft store, always read the label wrapped around the ball for more important details about the yarn you are considering. You may find that some will indicate that it is better for certain crafts than others.

Reading a yarn label can be a challenge for those that have never looked at one before. Below are some tips on how to decipher the yarn label code:

1. **The Largest Letters**—The letters or words dominating the label is the name of the company.

2. **Net Weight**—This indicates the bulk of the yarn: light, medium, or bulky. Look for the number "4" on the label. This indicates it is medium. "0" is for lace, "1" and "2" are fine, and "3" is light. "5" and "6" are bulky, and "7" indicates a jumbo weight.

3. **Length**—This is the total amount of yarn you will get in a ball. Make sure to check that the length is equal to or more than the project you are planning. If it is not, you will need to pick up more balls.

4. **Color and Color Number**—Typically, there is a name given to the color. It can be generic like "Bright Red" or more creative like "Robin Red Breast." There is a more specific color number associated with the color like "A432." If you are purchasing more than one ball of yarn for a project, double check that the color and color name are the same. The color may appear to be similar, but when you start to mix the two balls, you will notice any subtle differences. It is best to do a little check here to avoid a disaster later.

5. **Dye Lot**—Similar to checking the color name and number, this Dye Lot number indicates that the yarn was colored in the same batch. Again, this can slightly alter the color of the yarn even if they have the same color name and number. This will be listed as a simple combination of numbers like "567."

6. **Fiber Content**—This number and name will be given together. It will appear as a single fiber and percentage, such as "100% wool," or a combination of fibers and percentages, such as "50% acrylic, 50% wool." When beginning for many projects, stick to more natural fibers like wool and avoid acrylic because they will split and slip on your needles. Also, even though cotton is a natural fiber, it does not have much stretch and can be hard for a beginner to work with.

7. **Gauge and Laundry Symbols**—Sometimes, the care instructions will be given to you in words and sometimes in images only.

Not all companies provide all this information or in this way, but you will find a lot of it on most commercial yarns. Here is a sample yarn label for you to see some of the information described above:

One key symbol provided that is especially important for all knitters, including the advanced ones, is with the crossed knitting needles. This is typically a rectangle or square with two knitting needles crossed inside and a lot of numbers and letters placed around it. This little box tells you what knitting gauge and needle size you need. The center where the needles are crossed has a number written above it, for example, "4.5 mm." This is what knitting needle size the company recommends for this yarn. Below this may be another number like "7 US," which indicates the US knitting needle size, in the event, you are shopping and there is no millimeter measurement. To the left of the box are numbers such as "4X4 IN" and on top numbers such as "10X10 CM." This is information about the gauge swatch you need to make. It should be 4 inches wide and 4 inches long or 10 centimeters long and wide. The bottom of the box has a number and letter such as "20 S," and the right of the box has a number and letter such as "26 R." This information is about the stitches and rows. The bottom number and letter tell you that you should get 20 stitches ("S") and 26 rows ("R") into the 4-inch square. If there is another box next to it with a single hook, this is information for crocheting.

Below is an image for you to visually see the label:

It is a good practice to save your yarn label with the swatch you created, so you remember all the information and have the care instructions. If you are giving the project as a gift, include the yarn label so the recipient knows how to care for their new, beautiful present.

If you are not certain about the laundry symbols on the label, below is a cheat sheet to help you decipher the information:

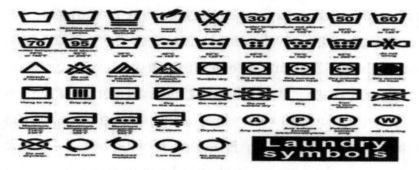

How to Pick Your Needles

You may notice that there are hundreds of different options when it comes to knitting needles. They come in all sorts of sizes and materials. Some people swear by bamboo or wood needles, while others love metal, such as aluminum, ones. Others enjoy the variety and economic benefit of plastic needles. As you continue practicing and trying out different tools, you will develop a preference, just like every knitter.

To begin, select a couple of different needles in different sizes to try out. Do not shy away from the curved, circular needles either. These may end up being your best friend. Circular needles do allow you to knit flat and can actually hold a lot more stitches than flat needles. This is especially handy for large projects. Many knitters love working with wooden needles, especially in the beginning, because of the strength and slight give in the material. They also grip the yarn well, unlike smooth options like some plastics and most metals.

Just as suggested to start with medium yarn, start knitting with medium-sized needles. Check for sizes like 6 US, 7 US, or 8 US. If the needles do not have US sizes on them, choose 4 mm, 4.5 mm, or 5 mm. These are best for medium yarns and feel good in your hands. This also applies to the thickness of the needle. Thin needles are great for thinner yarn while thicker needles compliment a thick yarn better. If you have a medium-weight wool yarn, choose a needle with medium thickness.

Another consideration is the needle length. This mainly applies to straight needles, but you will find the needles range in size from 7 inches up to 14 inches. Children typically use the smaller needles, but you may like the shorter sizes in the beginning. Shorter needles can be less difficult to maneuver and easier to use. If a project is large, however, choose a longer needle so it can hold more stitches.

When you choose the pattern, you wish to knit and the yarn you will be using to complete the project, choose a needle that corresponds to the pattern instructions and wool label as described above. Do not attempt to knit with a different sized needle than the pattern and wool calls for, especially if you are doing a clothing. This will result in an ill-fitting final project and can be frustrating after all the time and effort you put into it. There is a huge difference between the needle sizes, so make sure it all matches before you begin your project. It takes some attention to the details, but it is worth it in the long run!

Below is a small needle conversion chart to help you when you are purchasing needles so you can quickly determine if the needle will fit your project needs:

Metric/mm	US	Canadian/UK
2	0	14
2.25 OR 2.5	1	13
2.75	2	12
3.0	XX	11
3.25	3	10
3.5	4	XX
3.75	5	9
4.0	6	8
4.5	7	7
5.0	8	6
5.5	9	5

6.0	10	4
6.5	10.5	3
7.0	10.75	2
7.5	XX	1
8.0	11	0

- Knit and Purl

It is possible to create wonderful textures and patterns simply by alternating knitting and purling. Just remember to move your working strand back and forth so that it is in the right position for the stitch you are about to make. In other words, if you have just completed a purl stitch and the pattern calls for the next one to be knitted, move the yarn from the front (for purling) between the two needles and to the back (for knitting). If you DON'T move the yarn, you will end up with nasty, gaping holes from the yarn wrapping around your needle. The knit side is the "V" and the purl side is the horizontal bar (or what I call "the bump").

Where It Fits

Knit and purl stitch patterns can be used to make almost anything, such as sweaters, hats, scarves, mittens, bags, afghans and pillows. Guernsey (also known as "Gansey") is a traditional style of knitting that integrates these knit-purl combinations. You can use any weight of yarn but try to use simple fibers so you can see the pattern. The more texture or color variations in the yarn, the less of a pattern you will see in your fabric.

Knit to Purl stitches create a rib effect which looks amazing and I very often used for garments such as cardigans.

It's easy to recognize which is the purl and which is the knit stitch. The purl stitches have a horizontal bar (a small bump) under the stitch on the needle, whereas the knit stitches do not. Watch Changing Between Knit and Purl Stitches

- Bind off

Standard Bind-off

This method is the commonest of the bind-off techniques. Many knitters think this is the only method of binding off that can be done when knitting. If you desire to create an edge that will be sown into seams, use the standard bind-off method. The steps to making the standard bind-off are described below.

1. Move one stitch from the left-hand needle to the right-hand needle without twisting it. Then, knit one stitch.

2. Insert the tip of the left needle into the first stitch on the right needle.

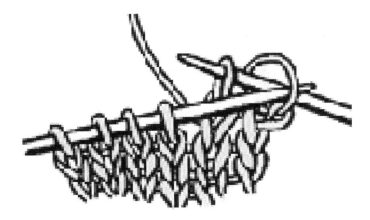

3. On the right needle, move the first stitch over the one next to it. Then, take them off the needle.

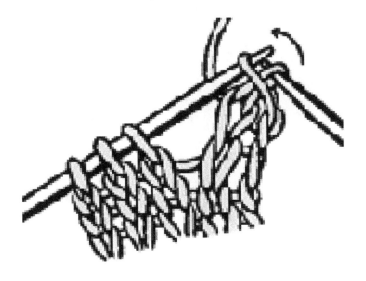

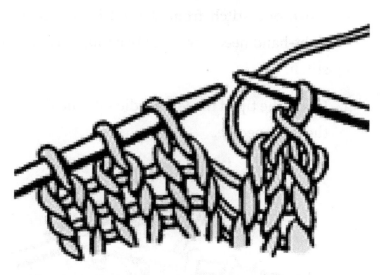

Following the steps above, on the right needle, one stitch has been bound-off and one stitch is left. To bind-off additional stitches, repeat the last two steps above. When the standard bind-off method is used, the end product looks like this

Invisible Ribbed Bind-off

When this method of bind-off is used, the edge produced is usually round and really elastic. Thus, it is suitable for neckbands. This bind-off is typically done with a tapestry needle. The steps to making an invisible ribbed bind-off are discussed below.

1. Measure the width of the material to be bound off. Then, cut yarn that is about 3 times that size, and thread the yarn onto a tapestry needle.

2. Pull the yarn through after inserting the tapestry needle from right to left through the first knit stitch.

3. Pull the yarn through after bringing the tapestry needle behind the knit stitch and inserting it from left to right into the second stitch.

4. From left to right, remove the first stitch from the knitting needle using the tapestry needle.

5. Pull the yarn through after inserting the tapestry needle into the next stitch from right to left.

6. From left to right, slip the first stitch off the knitting needle. Then, pull the yarn through after inserting the tapestry needle, from left to right behind the knit stitch, into the purl stitch after it.

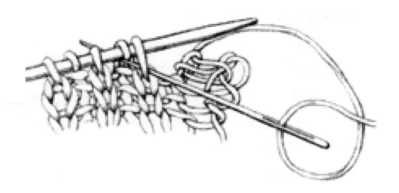

Repeat the last 3 steps to bind-off additional stitches. When invisible ribbed bind-off method is used, the end product looks like this

Sewn bind-off

Elizabeth Zimmermann invented this bind-off approach; hence, it is also referred to as Elizabeth Zimmermann's bind-off. When this bind-off method is used, the edges formed are exceedingly elastic. As such, the technique is excellent for projects that have a ropy appearance like toe-up socks. Like the invisible ribbed bind-off, this method is worked with a tapestry needle. The steps to making a sewn bind-off are highlighted below.

1. Measure the width of the material to be bound off. Then, cut yarn that is about 3 times that size, and thread the yarn onto a tapestry needle.

2. Pull the yarn through after inserting the tapestry needle from right to left through the first two stitches.

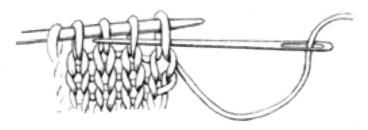

3. To remove the stitch from the needle, bring it from left to right through the first stitch and pull the yarn through.

Repeat the last two steps to cast off additional stitches. When sewn bind-off method is used, the end product looks like this

Chapter 3: Basic Techniques

Some people say there are several types of knitting stitches; however, there is really only one knit stitch with variations to it. This includes the purl stitch that you probably have heard a bit about already! It really is just a version of a traditional knit stitch. So, rest easy, you only have to master one stitch and then have fun learning how to mix it up a little bit

Keep your distance from the bedazzled choices of yarn. These are not good starter yarns. Instead, buddy up to the basic options. Flex your creative muscle with a bold color choice if you have a hard time accepting the simplicity at this point but try to keep the color light. The important thing is that you see your stitches as you practice, and a lighter yarn color will make it more apparent when you miss a stitch or make a mistake. Worsted weight wool is one of the most basic options you can go with.

- Stocking stitch

Skill Level: Beginner

Yarn: Any

Needle: Straight Type

Tools: N/A

The Stockinette Stitch is made up of knit and purl stitches. This stitch has a much smoother appearance than the Garter stitch but has the tendency to curl, so it's better suited to rolled cuff and rolled edged scarves.

When creating the Stockinette Stitch, it is important to remember that there is a 'right side' and a 'wrong side'. On the 'right side' the stitch will have the appearance of 'v' shapes.

Step 1 - Cast on and knit all of the stitches in the first row.

Step 2 - Swap the needles so that the needle with the stitches is back in your left hand.

Step 3 - Purl the next row of stitches.

Step 4 - Swap the needles again and knit the next row.

Step 5 - Continue to alternate until you have completed the appropriate number of stitches.

Step 6 - Once you have finished, then bind off to finish the project.

- Garter st

The Garter Stitch Scarf

To start this project, grab a set of knitting needles and a ball or two of yarn and cast on. Keep knitting back and forth with garter stitches and bind off when you are done. If you want to try another version, consider changing up the stitch to a basic knit or purl. Follow the same basic instructions and create a couple simpler scarves.

Choosing a practice project like this allows you to try out your cast on and bind off skills, as well as perfect your knitting technique for some of the more basic knits.

The Stocking Knit Washcloth

An added practice project is the sticking knit washcloth. This can be an intimidating project. Do not worry if it starts to curl as you work, this is normal!

Here is a more detailed pattern and Instructions:

Supplies:

1 100% cotton yarn, 2.5 ounces skein

7 US knitting needle pair

Scissors

Gauge and size:

Gauge—20 S (stitches) and 27 R (rows) per 4 inches. Not critical but keep as close as possible. Tighter washcloths are preferred over looser knits, so try to keep it close to this gauge.

Size—12 ¼-inch wide x 11-inch long.

Instructions:

1. Cast on 61 stitches.

2. Row 1—Knit completely across the front side.

3. Row 2—Use a 1 x 1 rib knit, knit one stitch, and purl the next across the entire row.

4. Keep repeating Steps 2 and 3 until your yarn is almost gone. Bind off.

5. For the excess yarn, trim it away and weave in the loose ends. You are done!

- Seed st (moss)

The moss stitch – sometimes known as a seed stitch – is an easy to create stitch, which produces wonderfully complex looking results. Follow directions for how to complete a moss stitch pattern below.

The Moss or Seed stitch consists of single knits and purls that alternate horizontally and vertically. Like the garter stitch, the moss stitch lies flat, making it a good edging for a sweater border and cuffs. The knitted fabric also looks the same from both sides, making it a nice choice for scarves and other pieces of which both sides are visible.

Cast on an even number of stitches.

1. Row 1: Alternate between knitting 1 stitch and purling 1 stitch across the row.

2. Row 2: Alternate between purling 1 stitch and knitting 1 stitch across the row.

3. Repeat Rows 1 and 2 for pattern.

When working the moss or seed stitch, you alternate between knit and purl stitches in each row. The trick to creating the little "seeds" is to knit in the purl stitches of the previous row and purl in the knit stitches of the previous row.

Double Seed Stitch

Skill Level: Beginner

Yarn: Any

Needle: Straight Type

Tools: N/A

An even number of stitches should be cast on.

In the right-hand side of **Row 1**, Knit 1 and Purl 1 to the very end.

Repeat Row # 1 in **Row 2**.

In **Row 3**, purl 1 and Knit 1 and repeat to the very end.

Repeat Row # 3 in **Row 4**.

Make a repetition from rows 1 through to the 4th. Repeat from row 1 to 4 till the length you desire.

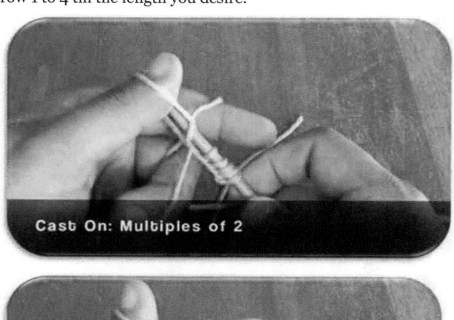

Cast On: Multiples of 2

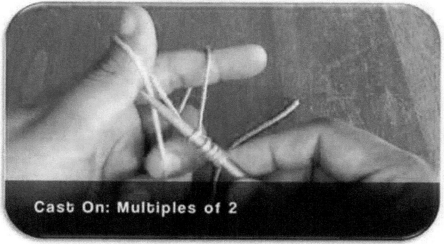

Cast On: Multiples of 2

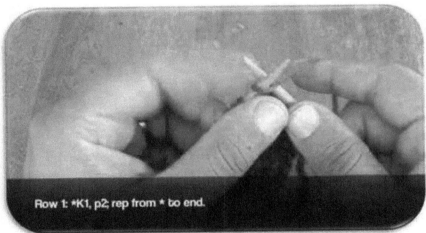

Row 1: *K1, p2; rep from * to end.

Row 1: *K1, p2, rep from * to end.

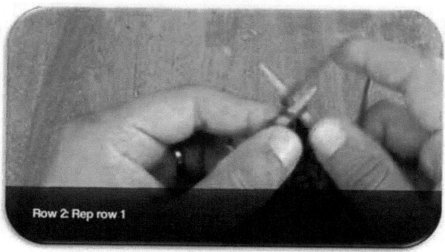

Row 2: Rep row 1

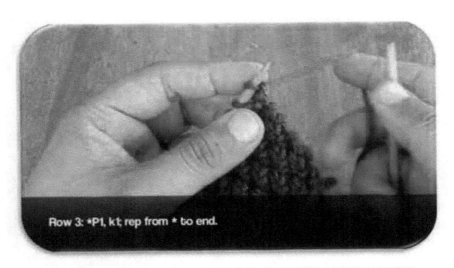

Row 3: *P1, k1; rep from * to end.

Row 3: *P1, k1; rep from * to end.

Row 4: Rep row 3

Row 4: Rep row 3

- Increase and Decrease

After learning the basics of knitting and purling, as well as the combination of both, you may want to add some spice by making subtractions and additions to your project. There are different methods of increasing and decreasing the stitches.

Knit in the Front and Back

1. Also known as "kfb", the knit in the front and back increase is done by first making a knit stitch. But keep the stitch from sliding off the left needle.

2. After you make a stitch on the right needle while the other stitch is still on the other left, finish the knit increase by knitting towards the back of the older stitch on the left needle. In the same way, the stitch being formed to the back is the same as on the front of the loop. You just did the knitting on the back part of the loop, behind the needle.

3. As soon as you get two stitches on the right needle, finish it by sliding the original stitch off the other needle. Now you have increased a single stitch.

Purl in Front and the Back

Also known as "pfb", the purl in front and the back is one way of increasing the stitches more easily. When you do a purl in front and back, you don't do it instinctively as when knitting although the technique is just similar.

In doing a purl in the front and the back, you also begin by purling stitches right through the loop in the front, having the stitch at the left needle. When purling through the back, simply loop the other needle around so you can work with it through the back loop in a left to right direction. These steps will feel quite awkward at first, but once you get used to it, you'd be making more purls on the side in no time.

Yarn Over

Doing a yarn over is also an efficient way for increasing stitches. This method produces a hold when knitting and is known as a combination for decreasing in 'knit two together'. This enables knitters to make sure that the number of stitches is similar across rows.

On the other hand, in producing a yarn over between two stitches, you have to wrap the right needle with the yarn in a back to front manner and a counterclockwise direction before starting every knit stitch. The stitches that follow are done as normal. When you make it to yarning over for the next row, do it in a normal stitch.

When you do a yarn over, it is just the same as when you are knitting or purling the following stitch. When you are knitting, you simply wrap the needle around the yarn and have it at the back. On the other hand, when purling, you have to wrap the needle with the yarn and have the yarn back in the front where it will be purled.

Make One

Also known as M1, 'make one' is a popular method for increasing knitting stitches. Make one left is abbreviated as M1L whereas make one right is abbreviated as M1R. This method is done in between stitches, and the bar also between stitches.

In making a M1L, get the left-hand needle and then pick the bar up from front to the back, in between stitches. Using your right needle, knit the bar using a back loop. On the other hand, to make a M1R, just lift the bar from the back to the front and knit the bar using a front loop.

Using the same stitches, you can do this by purling the side. Purl the back loop for a M1L and a front loop for a M1R.

Knit Two Together

A knit two together is the simplest method of decreasing the stitches. It decreases and makes a slight slant to the right and is usually combined with the SSK or the slip knit method, which is also used to decrease stitches and make a slant to the left, resulting to even decreases on both sides of the knitted piece. In knitting two together, it is like making a normal knit stitch. The only difference is that you work on two stitches instead of doing just one. Knit two together is also known as K2Tog.

Purl Two Together

As in knitting two together, you can also purl two together and get the same result on the purling side. In making a purl two together, just insert the right needle on the two loops on the left that follow, as if you were to purl. Do it in exactly the same way as you would do in a normal purl stitch. After doing two stitches, you now have one. The purl two together is also known as P2Tog.

Slip Knit

The slip knit is also a one of the simplest and most basic way for decreasing stitches. It makes a decrease and a slant to the left. It is usually used along with knit two together which creates a slant decrease to the right.

In doing a slip knit, just slip the very first stitch like you were going to knit, then slip again the second stitch as you were to knit. Then have the needle on the left slide to the front of the two stitches and do a knit stitch of both. Slip knit has an abbreviation of SSK.

- Casting Off

Casting off is also an important skill to learn, and this is done when you've completed either the project or that you're working on and need to get it completely off your needles. Binding off is another word for casting off, and you'll see both terms used in different patterns. Just remember not to do it too tightly if you want to continue later.

Start by knitting the first two stitches, and then insert the point of your left needle into the first stitch, pulling it over the second. The second stitch will then be off of your needle. This process should be continued until you're at the end of the row, and then you can pull the yarn through the last stitch, requiring you to pull it up, and leave a tail that's about six inches long. This will later be worked into your project. Take your tapestry needle, threading the tail through the stitches in a back and forth motion. This should make it where it can't be seen, and it'll keep your piece from unraveling.

- Long Tail Cast On

This method uses the tail end of the yarn to cast on and gives you a nice stretchy cast on. It is a good method for small to medium size projects since you have to estimate the amount of yarn you need for the cast on stitches. One way I do this is to cast on 10 stitches and then measure how much yarn I've used and figure out the length from there. Begin by holding the yarn with the tail end draped over your thumb and the end coming from the skein draped over your index finger and being held in the palm of your hand.

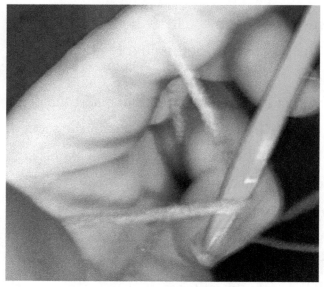

Take the needle and push the yarn between your index and thumb fingers down to form a V.

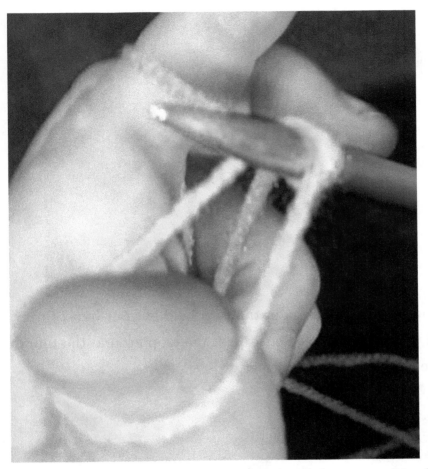

Bring the needle up through the loop formed on your thumb.

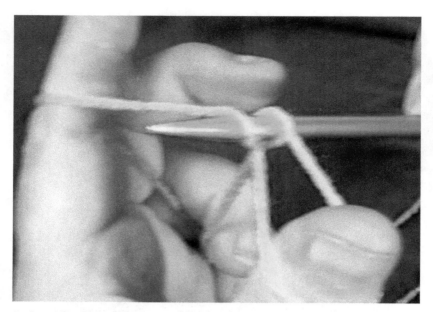

Bring the needle up under the yarn held by your index finger, and then pull the needle through the loop around the thumb once more and release the yarn.

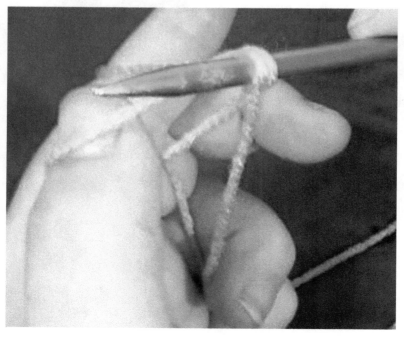

Two stitches are cast on first, and then one stitch are cast on after that. Repeat this process until you have the correct number of stitches cast on.

- Back Loop Cast On

The back loop cast on uses the yarn coming from the skein, and it gives you a slightly tighter cast on. Hold the yarn with the tail in the palm of your hand and draped over your index finger, and the yarn coming from the skein draped over your thumb. Draw the yarn down between your index and thumb with the knitting needle.

Bring the needle up through the loop on your thumb

Release the yarn and it will wrap around the needle.

- Knit on Cast On

One of the things I really like about this method is that it knits the first row for you. It produces a nice stretchy cast on which has a neat edge. Begin by placing a slip knot on the needle. Insert the right needle behind the slip knot on the left needle. Place the yarn over the right needle and draw the yarn through the slip knot. Do not slip the stitch onto the right needle but pull it out a bit and slip it back onto the left needle. You now have two stitches on the left needle. Continue to knit stitches slipping them onto the left needle until you have the correct number of casts on stitches.
Pull the stitch out a bit to give you room to work with it.
Slip the stitch back onto the left needle and snug it up.
Knit and Purl Stitches

- Knit Stitch

Hold the yarn in the back of your work insert the right needle into the back of the stitch on the left needle. Wrap the yarn around the right needle (called a yarn over) and draw the yarn through the stitch on the left needle. Pull the new stitch over onto the right needle. Repeat this process to knit the appropriate number of stitches.
Wrap the yarn around the right needle and pull it through the stitch on the left needle.

- Learn to Knit: 3 Basic Points

As in cooking, after talking about the ingredients of the recipe, knitting needles and balls of wool, now, we launch our popote with a zoom on the indispensable bases of the knitting, namely "by which points I start in knitting"?

The basic points

The Garter Stitch, The Base of Knitting

Yes, it's really the base. The one by which everyone starts! Why? Because it is easy to access and is a good entry point to the many possibilities of this creative hobby, and it is not by excess of enthusiasm that we tell you that, it is a reality!

In short, the foam point, what is it?

With the garter stitch, all the stitches and rows are knit in place. You flip over your knitting and on both sides, you see exactly the same points without distinction. Another very significant visual characteristic, the rendering "ripples". By knitting 2 consecutive rows, you form a wave.

It is very pretty, however, make regular wavelets, it is not a small matter. Do not doubt especially about you!

Irregularity can give birth to beauty, keep in mind that when you start, the garter stitch helps you take control of the needles and acquire the first automatisms of the great knitting artists.

The Jersey Point, This Undecided

After the garter stitch, the jersey stitch is the most common. They both knit with the same kind of needles.

But what is the difference with the foam stitch? Any simple! In stockinette, knit alternately a row of stitches and a row of stitches. At the visual level, it gives on the side of the place, "V", on the back of work, wavelets as in garter stitch.

Well, so far nothing complicated, is it? With just a little training and tenacity, these 2 techniques are really super easy to master. Childish!

If you already want to see and deepen the mesh knitting upside down, you can read this article.

Otherwise, we go to the ribs!

Knit in Ribs or The Art of Rhythmic Knitting

With the ribs, we alternate. A "place" shot, a "backwards" shot. In short, how is it going?

Well, you knit the first stitch of your model in the right place (like in garter stitch) then you slide the yarn between your 2 needles to put it in position "back stitch". It's a shot to take, it's true, but to repeat this movement gives dynamics to knitting, very nice. And then, making ribs greatly expands the possibilities in terms of creative patterns you'll see!

On a boss, the mention "ribs" is always accompanied by numbers: 1/1, 2/2, 4/2, ...

Qualco? Are we already going to knit double stitches? Well no! These are the indications on the sequence of the number of stitches up / down to achieve. A kind of musical sequence in which we repeat the same time.

For example:

1/1 = 1 stitch place then knit the next stitch upside down

2/2 = 2 stitches, and 2 stitches back. The first number always indicates the place. Logic!

To understand the technique and learn how to knit, the video tutorial on the ribs is there!

Other knit stitches also exist in this style, such as English ribs or beaded ribs. For the moment, trust us, it's too soon, we'll come back to it a little later in another article dedicated to the smooth learning of technical coasts.

Finally, a last little knitting board. If one day you do not know where you are, where you are, look where your knitting yarn is located:

Is he behind? You have just finished a stitch place, the next will be towards

he is in front? It's the opposite, you were doing a stitch, go to the place.

Chapter 4: Advanced techniques

- How cast on with circular needles

Circular needles were created during the early 1900s. They have straight tips connected to a flexible cable thus they can be used for knitting round and flat fabrics.

A thin cable joins together two short needles that vary in length. As opposed to knitting back and forth, these needles are used for knitting in a circular manner in the seamless round.

The length of the longer needle is suitable for knitting wider items such as Afghans. Scarves can also be knit with the circulars, since the two ends of the circulars can be used to get back and forth. The scarf can be left to loosely hang on the cable when not knitting and you therefore need not worry about the stitches slipping off. Circular needles are often used when knitting socks too, so throughout this book, you will become very familiar with them.

When you are working in the round, you will begin by casting on the required number of stitches, just as you would for flat knitting. Depending upon the needles you are using, your stitches may be on a single circular needle, divided between two circular needles, or spread between three or four double-pointed needles. If you are placing stitches on more than one needle, make sure the space between the needles is pulled quite snug. When you finish casting on your stitches, lay the work flat and carefully check for any twists between the stitches. Twisting the cast-on row will result in a ruined project and a frustrating fresh start.

Once you have completed your cast-on, the pattern will direct you to "join the work in the round," often with no other instructions. While you can begin knitting to join your work, this produces a slight jog or unevenness in your knitting and does not create the neatest finish. For a neat, more even and more secure join, holding the tips of the two needles near one another, slip the first cast on stitch over the last. Place the last stitch cast on onto the tip of the right-hand needle and the first onto the tip of the left-hand needle. The two stitches have swapped places. Place a stitch marker to mark the beginning of the round and start knitting according to your pattern. If you do not have a stitch marker, a loop of knotted contrasting yarn, small hair elastic, or even a snipped bit of a drinking straw will do! As an alternative you can also cast-on one additional stitch. Slip the first stitch cast-on onto the left-hand needle tip. Knit two together (see the increase and decrease for a how-to!) and place a marker to note the beginning of the round.

- Provisional cast on.

A provisional cast lets you knit in two directions. When creating a provisional cast on use either cotton or acrylic yarn as the provisional yarn so that it does not felt into your work. First knot the two yarns together. Hold the two yarns like you were going to do a long tail cast on. The working yarn should be toward you and the provisional yarn away from you.

Slide the needle under the working yarn, up and under both yarns, and under the working yarn again forming a cast on stitch. The working yarn will form the cast on stitches while the provisional yarn will be carried under the cast on stitches. When you are ready to knit leave the provisional yarn alone and only work with the working yarn.

When you are ready to work on the provisional cast on slide the needle into all of the loops of the working yarn. Once they are all on your needle you can undo the knot and separate the two yarns. Gently pull the provisional yarn out of the cast on stitches being careful not to let any of the cast on stitches fall off of your needle. If they do very carefully slide them back onto your needle. Now you are ready to start knitting from the other direction of the original cast on.

Slide the needle under the working yarn and then up and under both yarns.

Catch the working yarn and pull the provisional yarn to the left to create a cast on stitch.

A completed provisional cast on

Notice how the provisional yarn is resting in the working yarn's cast on stitches.

Begin by sliding the needle into the cast on loops and then gently removing the provisional yarn. Normally you would bind off the knitted project, but I left the needle in to take this picture. If you're not ready to bind off the thread a tapestry needle with contrasting yarn and thread it through the loops on the needle. Remove the needle and you can then work on your project and come back to this end and add more knitting.

- Raglan, top down, bottom up.

Take-it-easy Sweater

You'll be cozy and ready to relax in this comfortable sweater. There are always many steps involved in creating a sweater, so take your time and have fun!

Materials:

Worsted weight yarn, approximately 1300 yards

Size US 7 circular needles, 29" circumference

Back of sweater:

Cast on 80.

Work in reverse Stockinette stitch: purl every stitch, every row, until piece measures 13" from beginning.

Complete the following rows for armhole shaping:

Row 1: Bind off 5 stitches, purl to end.

Row 2: Bind off 5 stitches, purl to end.

Row 3: K2Tog, purl to next-to-last stitch, K2Tog.

Row 4: Purl.

Row 5: K2Tog, purl to next-to-last stitch, K2Tog.

Row 6: Purl.

Row 7: K2Tog, purl to next-to-last stitch, K2Tog.

Row 8: Purl.

Row 9: K2Tog, purl to next-to-last stitch, K2Tog.

Row 10: Purl.

Continue working in reverse Stockinette stitch until piece measures 22" from beginning.

Bind off.

Front of sweater:

Cast on 80.

Work in reverse Stockinette stitch: purl every stitch, every row, until piece measures 13" from beginning.

Complete the following rows for armhole and neck shaping:

Row 1: Bind off 5 stitches, purl to end.

Row 2: Bind off 5 stitches, purl to end.

Row 3: K2Tog, purl to next-to-last stitch, K2Tog.

Row 4: Purl.

Row 5: K2Tog, purl 32, knit 4, purl 32, K2Tog.

Row 6: Purl 31, knit 4, purl 31.

Row 7: K2Tog, purl 28, knit 2, pick up a new ball of yarn and bind off 1 stitch, use new ball of yarn for rest of row: knit 2, purl 27, K2Tog.

You will now be working the two sides of the neck separately with different balls of yarn.

Continue working in reverse Stockinette stitch until piece measures 20" from beginning, decreasing every other row by doing K2Tog as the first stitch, and knitting the two stitches edging the neckline. Bind off.

Sleeves (make 2):

Cast on 22.

Work in reverse Stockinette stitch (purl every stitch), working the increase row every 6th row 3 times, then working the increase row every 8th row for 4 times. Increase row: P1, M1, Purl across, M1, P1. Continue working in reverse Stockinette until piece measures 16" from beginning.

Complete the following rows for shoulder cap shaping:

Row 1: Bind off 4 stitches, purl to end.

Row 2: Bind off 4 stitches, purl to end.

Row 3: K2Tog, purl to end, K2Tog.

Row 4: Purl.

Row 5: K2Tog, purl to end, K2Tog.

Row 6: Purl.

Row 7: K2Tog, purl to end, K2Tog.

Row 8: Purl.

Row 9: Purl.

Repeat rows 7 – 9 twelve times.

Bind off 3 stitches of next four rows.

Bind off all remaining stitches.

Finishing:

Using mattress stitch, sew together:

Shoulder seams

Sleeve seams

Top of sleeve and armhole

Back and front pieces at each side

Weave in all yarn ends.

Use your fingers to loosely lace in an extra piece of yarn for a neck drawstring.

- Short rows (wrap and turn) sew on different kind of works.

Short rows are used for many things in knitting. You use them when knitting Entrelac and you can also use them to create a better fit in a garment. For example, if the pattern will be tight in the bust you can use short rows to help add more room in the bust and get a better fit.

Knit to where you want to insert short rows and turn your work. Slip the last stitch you knitted to the left needle. Bring the yarn to the front of the work, slip the stitch back onto the left needle, bring the yarn to the back and slip the stitch back to the right needle. This is called wrapping a stitch. Purl the amount of stitches you need and turn your work. Now you will wrap the first stitch. Pull the yarn forward, slip the first stitch onto the right needle, pull the yarn to the back and slip the stitch back to the left needle and knit the appropriate number of stitches.

When you come to the wrapped stitch slip at the end of the row slip the needle into both the wrap and the next stitch and knit them together. Knit across the row. Turn your work and purl. When you get to the wrapped purl stitch slip the wrap onto the left needle and purl both the wrap and the next purl stitch together. This hides the wrap and makes it invisible on the right side. Continue to purl across the row and continue with the pattern. - picking up and knit.

- Picking Up and Knit

Sometimes it is helpful to add stitches to the side or ends of your knitting. This is a really handy technique to use when you need to add something like a collar or a button placket. Simply insert the right needle under the stitch on the edge and wrap the yarn knit wise and pull it through the stitch. Insert the needle into the next stitch, wrap the yarn knit wise and pull it through onto your needle. Continue to do this until you have added as many stitches as you need. Turn the work and start to knit.

Be sure to catch two loops over the needle when picking up stitches. This creates a strong stitch that will not stretch out and form a hole in your work. You can also use this method to add stitches to the side of a project or anywhere you need to add stitches.

- Cables without a Cable Needle

Creating cables without a cable needle is not for the faint hearted. Well actually it's not that hard if you are creating small cables. What you are doing is crossing the stitches before you work them. For example if you are working a cable in which the knit stitches will be crossed in the back (2 knit stitches in back, 1 purl stitch in front) insert the left needle into the third stitch (the purl stitch) and gently pull it over the knit stitches letting them slip off the left needle. Slip the two knit stitch back onto the left needle, slip the purl stitch back onto the left needle, and then you can purl one and knit two creating a crossed cable.

To create the next leg of the crossed cable you will insert the needle into second and third stitch on the left needle knit wise (the two knit stitches) and pull them over the purl stitch letting the purl stitch slip off the needle. Slip the purl stitch back onto the left needle and slip the two knit stitches back onto the left needle. Now you can knit two stitches and purl one forming the next leg of the crossed cable.

Try not to move your work around when the stitches are not on a needle. This method works best when you only have a few stitches to cross. Larger crossed cables require a cable needle so that you don't lose stitches.

Chapter 5: Understanding Patterns.

- Knitting charts

As you advance, you will find that some patterns rely upon charts instead of written instructions or offer both charts and written instructions. Charts typically include both right and wrong side rows, typically starting with a right-side row, on row one or include both odd and even numbered rounds. Simpler charts may not include wrong side or even numbered rows, providing notations only for right side rows or odd numbered rounds. Wrong side rows or even numbered rounds may be knitted or purled, according to the instructions.

You must read row one from right to left, not left to right. If you are working in the round, you will read both odd and even numbered rows on the chart from right to left. When working flat, right side rows will be worked from right to left and wrong side rows from left to right on the chart. Charts are most often repeated. You may for example have a chart displaying eight rows, with instructions to repeat the chart four to six times.

Knitting charts are made up of a variety of symbols. A key in the pattern will identify what each symbol means, from a basic knit or purl to an increase or decrease. In some instances, the same symbol may have a different meaning on right and wrong side rows. For example, a blank square may indicate a knit stitch on the right side and a purl stitch on the wrong side. Review the key and try to visualize the pattern in your head to reduce mistakes. If the pattern includes both a chart and a written version, you may find it helpful to read through both the chart and written pattern to fully understand what you are knitting.

Colorwork charts may be printed in color, rather than symbols. It may also rely on both symbols and color or just symbols. If your colorwork chart uses symbols, taking the time to color the chart with colored pencils can be helpful. There are several different types of colorwork; they include fair isle, intarsia and duplicate stitch. All use similar charts. When you are first working with charts, you may find it helpful to maintain careful notes that track which row you are on or you can use a piece of paper or removable tape to track your progress on the chart. These tricks are also helpful for more experienced knitters working on challenging charts, like lace patterns.

- Knitting glossary terms.

If you have ever been at a location where knitting is being done, you may have heard words like 'cast-on,' 'bind-off,' among others. Now that you want to begin to knit, you need to know the terms commonly used when knitting so that you will understand when other knitters use them. Highlighted and explained below are standard knitting terms you should be familiar with as you begin knitting.

Knitting Term	Meaning
Alternate	Knit every other row
Attached I Cord (also referred to as I cord)	A knitted cord-like, thick tubing for edging, borders, and hems, usually made with double-sided knitting needles
Backstitch	A stitch used to join two pieces together. It is generally made along a hem on a straight line
Backstitch seam	A seam stitch used to join two pieces of knitted works together

Backward loop cast-on	A simple and common type of casting on that contains a chain of half stitches and a slip knot
Bind-off	To complete a knitting project by concluding with a final row that consists of two stitches slipped over each other until one last stitch remains, and then the yarn is cut and looped through the remaining single stitch
Bind-off knit	Used to conclude the edge of knitted materials. Usually, one would knit each loop before moving it to the next.
Bind-off purl	Used to conclude the edge of knitted materials. Usually, one would purl each loop before moving it to the next.
Blanket stitch	A stitch containing widely spaced, intertwining purls or loops
Blocking	Used to conclude the edge of knitted materials. Usually, one would purl each loop before moving it to the next.

Bobble	Several stitches created in a particular spot on a knitted fabric that gives a ball-like or bumps decoration
Cable cast-on	A method of making the first set of stitches in a knitting project where a denser, corded edge is created by drawing a new loop over two previous loops and adding them to the needle
Cables	Cordlike decorative knitting patterns made by crossing several stitches over another
Cast-on	To create the foremost stitch that forms the background for a knitting work
Continental knitting	A knitting style where the knitter holds the yarn with the non-dominant hand
Couching stitch	A method of stitching in which the yarn is fastened down with tiny stitches to the top of a knitted project

Cross stitch	A method of stitching where duos of diagonal stitches of similar length are made to cross one another in the center to form a '+' or 'x' shape
Daisy stitch	A method of stitching used to create petals of a flower
Decrease	A knitting instruction which signifies reducing the amount of stitches by a particular number
Double cross stitch	A method of making stitches where two cross stitches are added to an already made cross stitch to give a design with 8 points
Double point needles	Knitting needles with pointed edge on both sides
Drop stitch	A stitching method that utilizes additional loops around a working needle to give the project an airy and light impression
Duplicate stitch	A stitching method to emphasize or add dimension a particular aspect of a knitting project by duplicating a stitch on another

English knitting	A knitting style where the yarn is held in the right hand
Frogging	The process of unscrambling already made stitches, probably due to a mistake
Garter stitch	A stitching style that involves using knit for every row and every stitch
Gauge	The number of rows and stitches needed during knitting to get the accurate size of a finished knitted material
Increase	To upsurge the number of stitches for knitting a project by a particular number as stated in the knitting instruction
Intarsia	A knitting technique pictures and designs are illustrated with colored yarns within a knitting project
Jogless join	A process of seamlessly altering colors within a knitting project

Kitchener stitch (also referred to as grafting)	This is a stitching method where two separate knitting pieces that are yet to be finally bound off are joined to create a subtle seam at the two edges
Knit	This is the act of making stitches
Knit 2 together	A method for decreasing stitches that involves inserting the needle simultaneously into two stitches; thereby, treating them as one
Knit stitch	This is the most basic stitch in the knitting craft
Knitted cast-on	A method of laying the foundation for the entire knitting project where the knit stitch is used for the cast-on
Lifted increases	A method of knitting where stitches are subtly added to a project, one at a time, so the finished technique is nearly invisible
Live stitch	A stitch that is still being worked on.

Long-tail cast-on	A cast-on method where the knitter begins with a lengthy tail of yarn and creates stitches that combine the other side of the yarn as well as the tail
Loop cast-on	A method of casting on which involves making loops and sliding them to the needle
Magic loop	A knitting method usually used for circular projects like socks, hats, among others. Knitters accomplish this, more often than not, by using circular needles
Mattress stitch seam	This is a stitch for joining two knitted materials along their edges such that the seam is almost unnoticeable
Moss stitch	A method of knitting where one purl stitch and one knit stitch are alternated in every row
Pick up and knit	A process of adding stitches to an already completed knitted material

Provisional cast-on	A cast-on method which involves creating a continuum without boundaries by pulling the waste yarn from the initial casting on. Thereby allowing the knitter to continue knitting in the opposite direction
Purl	Aside from the knit stitch, the purl is the most popular kind of stitch that is used in knitting. It is achieved by inserting the right needle into the front of the left needle to make a stitch.
Purl 2 together	This is a method of reducing stitches that involves combining two stitches to become one by purling two loops from the left needle
Repeat	To follow the previous instruction again
Reverse I cord	This is a method similar to the I cord, but it requires the yarn to be pulled up towards the knitted material's front

Reverse Shaping	This is a process that involves shaping a knitted material on the second side, beginning from where the initial shaping on the main side stopped. More often than not, this includes binding off
Ribbing	This requires combining purl and knit stitches in a single row to create a stretch fabric that is suitable for neck holes and sleeves
Row	This is used to describe a series of stitches that have been completed from one working needle to the other.
Running stitch	An over-and-under or straight stitch which can run vertically, diagonally or horizontally across a knitted material
Satin stitch	A series of flat stitches embroidered close together on top of knitted materials, usually used to make embellishments and decorative designs

Selvage	The edges of the first and last knitted rows, also called the raw edge of a knitted material
Sewn bind-off	This bind-off type requires the knitter to leave a tail of yarn which is sewn through the stitches when they are dropped. Thereby creating a clean, finished edge. It is most suitable for top up socks and neck edges
Slip	To move a stitch that was previously on the left needle to the right needle without adding yarn
Slip knot	This is the first design made with the yarn to commence a knitting project. It is the first stitch
Slip Stitch	A method of eliminating purl or knit stitch where a stitch is moved from one needle to the other
Slip, slip, knit	A process of reducing stitches by slipping, this slants to the left

Slip, slip, purl	A process of reducing stitches by purling, this slants to the right
Straight stitch	This is made by alternating between a row of purl stitches and a row of knit stitches. It is also referred to as stockinette stitch
Tink	This means to fix a mistake made during a knitting project by unknitting back to the affected stitch and correcting it. This kind of fix is not recommended for entire rows, only for short distances
Work even	This is a knitting instruction that means to work the pattern straight without any increase or decrease to the stitch. It also includes an instruction not to shape
Yarn Back	To put a front-sitting yarn to the back
Yarn forward	To bring a back-sitting yarn to the front

- Knitting project

As a knitting beginner, you may go crazy about getting all those beautiful stuff from your craft supply store and grab all those that look fancy to you. However, it makes sense to use only a few of these supplies and materials when just getting started to knit. It is certainly reasonable to only purchase a few materials for practice because you may not like the quality of yarns you got or the type of needles you use. It is recommended to start exploring materials after a few practices.

As a beginner, you do not actually need the most expensive materials. You can find great supplies at a discount in so many arts and crafts store. All you need are the simplest supplies for practice.

So, what will you need for knitting? Let's go through these, one by one.

1. Knitting yarn

To start with a knitting project, you will need a knitting yarn. To have a good knit, you must make sure you have chosen the right yarn. It should be selected based on which works best for the clothing you are about to make, and which coordinates well with other materials. In most cases, when just starting a project as a beginner, a consideration of which supplies fit together is not a requirement. However, it may be useful when already knitting clothes later on. Simple wears such as scarves, shawls, or blankets may not require much difference in which kind of yarn one should use. But knit wears such as sweaters require that you first determine a pattern before selecting what yarn to use. After the selection of pattern, beginners must use the recommended yarn as failure to do so may spoil your knit-wear creation.

So, when choosing a yarn, you should determine first which type of project you will begin with, whether you are making simple ones or knit wears. Once you have picked a project, you can ask yourself a few questions. What weight of the yarn should I be using for this project? How much yarn is needed to complete this? Does it require an ordinary yarn or a novelty yarn? Does it work better with a specific fiber?

When you already have an idea of which yarn to use, you will no longer be overwhelmed with all those elaborate and colorful yarns in the local store. You can have your fingers do the testing. Determine the appropriate yarns by getting a feel of it and see if it fits what you want for your project. But if you have set yourself on a certain yarn, it would still make sense to look for patterns which work best for that type of yarn. Or in another way, you may look for a pattern that works well with your chosen yarn. It works just the same.

2. Knitting needles

Knitting needles or knitting pins are also important materials needed for a knitting project. A knitting needle is a long stick used to stitch fabrics or knit wears. Today, knitting is done using two needles, but historically, it was done using only a single needle. Despite the presence of many knitting machines which enable easier and faster creation of knit wears, many people still opt to knit the old way.

Knitting needles are used to get through the stitches and make series of loops. This process is repeated all throughout. Knitting needles are best when they are very smooth, thin, and very long enough to reach the stitches. The needles should also be sturdy to avoid from bending or breaking while in the process of stitching.

In choosing a knitting needle, you may find them in different sizes and of different materials, from aluminum, to bamboo sticks, or rosewood. These are ideal needles and very nice to have when sticking to the traditional knitting method, but as a beginner, it would be fine to use either needles made of aluminum or plastic. Choosing a knitting needle would depend on many factors. It would usually depend on which yarn is used in the project, or what kind of fabric is needed to be produced. The kind of pattern to follow will also be a determining factor.

When just starting out, you may likely be buying needles of different sizes for every project, but that would be alright, so you could see how you like each needle size.

3. Sewing needles

The sewing needles are used in weaving the ends of your knit-wears. It is also used in putting up the parts of garments together, such as the sleeves of knit wears. There are sewing needles in plastic or metal which are comfortable to use with yarns. Always make sure to choose the needles with large eyes or holes so that the yarn can easily get through.

4. Crochet hooks

Sometimes, knitting garments may require crochet hooks. The crochet hooks are handy tools which are essential especially when the yarn ends are too short to be tied using the sewing needle. The sizes G and H are good for almost all weights of yarn and are the easiest to use.

When you have all these tools for knitting, then you are ready for your first project. There are many tools needed for knitters, but these are the basic ones that will help you get started with your first knitting project.

Chapter 6: Knitting patterns.

- For Beginner

As a beginner knitter, you may find it challenging reading knitting patterns. What you will likely see is a coded writeup, filled with abbreviations. But I need to tell you that reading a knitting pattern is not exactly difficult.

A knitting pattern is a set of written instructions that tell the knitter how to make a knitted fabric.

We will discuss how to read and understand knitting patterns. But first, let's consider the typical set of information that is encoded into a knitting pattern.

Necessary Pieces of Information on a Knitting Pattern

• **Skill Level**: More often than not, this is the first information that is included in a knitting pattern after the name and picture of the knitted material. This is great for beginner knitters, because you can know the materials that you should attempt and those you shouldn't try to knit. For instance, when you see 'intermediate' or 'advanced' on a pattern, you simply skip it till you have become an intermediate or advanced knitter, respectively.

- **Size**: The size of the project is only essential if you are making a material that needs to fit on the user. However, for a start, you will be working with projects that don't need to fit precisely on the wearer. Such projects include scarves, blankets, among others. As you become a more professional knitter, you should check the size of the fabric before knitting.

- **Gauge**: Like size, the gauge is not essential for projects that don't require fitting on the user. However, to learn more about gauge.

- **Yarn and needle sizes**: This will tell you the size and type of yarn and knitting needles that were used in the project, as well as any other special tools that you will need during the project. You don't need to use the exact type of yarn that was used in the project. You can use yarn of similar weight or thickness.

- Abbreviations: More often than not, abbreviations are used to denote instructions in knitting patterns.

- For Intermediate

Intermediate patterns may be constructed simply but include more detailed knitting. Such as simple cable patterns, basic lace, colorwork. It also includes projects that can be simply knitted but include more complex shaping. Once you have successfully handled some easy knitting projects, you can move on to a more challenging project that matches your taste. If you are excited about lace, consider a classic rectangular scarf, rather than a triangular or circular shawl. Sweater knitters should choose a simple cardigan, rather than a heavily cabled one as they master the skills required.

- For Expert

Advanced patterns combine the skills mastered while completing simple and intermediate projects. These projects frequently use complex shaping, along with colorwork, lace and cables. Even experienced knitters need to pay attention to these projects and they are best saved for focused knitting time.

Chapter 7: Tips and Tricks.

1. Make sure you take plenty of breaks while you are knitting. The repetitive movement can cause or worse carpal tunnel. Make sure you are stretching your hands and giving them a break from the constant movement.

2. Just as you have to move your hands you have to move your body. Often times we get caught up in our projects working on them for hours at a time. You need to make sure you are getting up and moving around at least once an hour. This will help make sure your neck, back and arms do not start hurting. You also need to make sure you are getting enough exercise and not just knitting all day because this can lead to weight gain.

3. Have a plan as to where you will store all of your knitting supplies. If you leave your supplies laying all over the house, you will find that your yarn gets tangled and your needles get bent or lost. One way I store my yarn is by using a behind the door shoe rack. This allows me to place all of my yarn in slots (where shoes would normally go) and keep my

needles as well as scissors and other supplies up where children can't reach them.

4. Don't go crazy buying a bunch of knitting supplies when you first start out. As you learn how to knit, you will find that you like specific things such as bamboo needles or a specific brand or texture of yarn. You don't want to waste money when you are starting out on things you will never use.

5. Always make sure that the yarn you are choosing goes with the project you are making. For example, if you are making a scarf for a child you want a yarn that is durable but if you are making a blanket for a baby you don't want that same durable yarn you want something soft and cuddly.

6. Make sure that you are using the same type of yarn for your projects. Often times you will run out of yarn and have to go pick up some more, the store may be out of the brand you were using so you choose another brand. When this happens, you need to make sure if you started with yarn that could be machine washed you don't pick up a yarn that needs to be hand washed. This is also important to remember then you are changing colors.

7. When you are following a pattern, you need to make sure you are using the proper gauge yarn as well as

the proper size needles. These patterns do not give any room for using a different yarn or needle so if you are making a sweater and use the wrong needle or yarn you will find it does not come out the correct size.

8. Plan ahead and tie in new yarn at the end of a row. Of course, you can tie the yarn in at the middle of a row, but it is much easier to hide the sewn in ends if you end at the end of a row. You will need about four times the length of a row in yarn per row. So, if you are finishing up a row and know you will not be able to finish another one before needing more yarn go ahead and add it in at the end of the row.

9. Make sure you are not knitting at the top of you knitting needle. If you look at your needle you will see the top is much thinner than the rest of your needle. This will make your stitches far too small and not only hard to work with, but it will cause you project to look awkward.

10. Don't mix the textures of your yarn when working on a project. Many people think they can create a blanket or throw by using a bunch of different yarns that they have no use for. Don't mix yarn sizes or textures this does not produce a nice piece of work.

Instead save that yarn for a smaller project such as dish cloths or coasters.

That is all I have for you, but the most important thing I can tell you is to make sure you enjoy the process of learning how to knit. Many people try to learn how to knit but they get frustrated and give up early on. If you become frustrated, just walk away from the project and come back to it later with a clear mind. You can't imagine what a difference it is when you have a clear mind and are ready to work on your project again.

Some Tips to Get Started

You already know that you want to knit, and you know how. You even have some projects that you can start with, and some are harder than others. Of course, that doesn't mean you aren't still a little intimidated. It can be hard to jump right in there, and it can be frustrating if you're worrying about every little thing. This is dedicated to tips to help you succeed and feel a little more confident with your newfound skill.

Tip #1 Stick with Inexpensive Yarn

This may seem like a no-brainer, but it's something that you should really try out. When you go to pick up supplies, you may get overwhelmed by all of the choices. Some of them are bound to be more expensive than others, and some are even harder to work with. Remember that inexpensive yarn, especially manmade yarn, is considered to be easy to work with, and so it should be picked up first.

Of course, another reason that you'd want to pick up inexpensive yarn at first is because yarn will be wasted, and mistakes will be made. If you've already sunk a lot of money into a project and then just put a lot of time and effort into it as well, then you're going to feel like you've wasted a lot more. This could lead to you feeling discouraged, and that's the last thing you need if you want to become a knitting pro.

Tip #2 Keep Your Abbreviations Handy

In this book, your abbreviation chart isn't really needed for the most part. However, when you start to work with other patterns, it's important to keep that abbreviation list on hand if you want to truly keep going. You aren't always going to want to stop, look for it, and then continue what you were doing all over again. Having it on hand makes it easy to glance over and start to memorize everything that's needed to go in an easy flowing manner.

Tip #3 Knit with Others

You may feel a little insecure about this tip at first because you're just beginning, but when you're sitting down to knit, it's best not to do it alone. This isn't true for everyone, but a lot of people find that it's a hobby that they'll keep for longer and excel at more if they have more people helping them along and encouraging them.

Knitting with a friend is a great bonding activity, and it allows you something to do when you run out of ideas or want a nice day or night in with someone that you care about. You can even bounce ideas off of each other and help when the other person is having trouble, making mistakes less likely to happen in the first place.

Tip #4 Get Decent Scissors

Once again, this may seem a little obvious, but you don't want to get the cheapest or oldest pair of scissors out there. It's important that you get a decent pair of scissors that won't fray the yarn that you're working on. Some yarn can be broken or cut in this way without repercussion, but a good pair of scissors will often save you a lot of trouble later down the road.

Tip #5 Take it Easy

It's important not to want everything to work out too quickly. Take it easy with your first project and start with the simpler ones that you find in this book. Even after you're done with these seven projects, you're still going to want to make sure that you stick with easier projects at first until you feel a little more confident. Otherwise, you may end up over your head with no one to turn to. Practicing your basics will pave the way for a lot of fancier projects down the road, which you'll then be able to complete with pure confidence.

Tip #6 Organize Your Supplies

You may not be the most well-organized person in the world, but there should be some organization to your supplies if you want to knit without any added frustration. Always having to look for something is sure to frustrate you, and it may cause you to give up on a project entirely. You'll want everything where it's easily found and accessible. Having a knitting bag or basket beside you when you start is always a good recommendation and having an organized one will be even better. It'll even keep you from losing the things that you need to finish, saving you money on supplies in the long since you won't have to rebuy anything. It'll also save you time so that you'll be able to complete your projects in a much timelier manner.

Chapter 8: Intermediate Knitting Stitches and Project

Hopefully, you are all hyped up at graduating to the intermediate level and are chomping at the bit to get going on a new pattern. Do not hold back! Try out one of these stitches in a previous pattern or give the pattern at the bottom a shot. Enjoy and keep those needles moving!

Stitches

Give some of these stitches a try in a last project. They are fun and different. Consider replacing all the "beginner" parts of the pattern or just adding a few rows of one of these new stitches. They are sure to add some flair.

Quilted Diamond

1. Cast on 13 stitches at a minimum. Increase by multiple of 10 as needed.

2. Row 1—Repeat the pattern of purl 3 and knit 1, moving the yarn over and ending by knitting 1 stitch across the length of the row.

3. Step 2 creates a double row of stitching, and it adds 2 stitches for each repeat.

4. Rows 2 and 3—Purl 3 and knit 3, repeating the pattern across the row.

5. Row 4—Purl 3 together and knit 3, repeating the pattern across the row.

6. Row 5—Purl all the stitches across the row.

7. Row 6—Knit all the stitches across the row.

8. Row 7—Purl 1, knit 1, move the yarn over, and knit 1. Repeat this pattern across the row.

9. Row 8—Knit 2, purl 3, and knit 3. Repeat the purl 3 and knit 3 patterns until you reach the last 4 stitches. Finish by purling 3 and knitting 1.

10. Row 9—Purl 1, knit 3, and purl 3. Repeat the knit 3 and purl 3 pattern until you reach the last 5 stitches. Finish by knitting 3 and purling 2.

11. Row 10—Knit 2, purl 3 together, and knit 3. Repeat purl 3 together and knit 3 until you reach the last 4 stitches. Finish but purling 3 together and knitting 1.

12. Repeat Steps 2 through 11 as desired.

Basket Weave

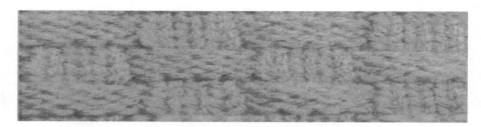

1. Cast on 13 stitches at a minimum. Increase by multiple of 8 as needed.

2. Rows 1 and 5—On the right side, knit across the row.

3. Rows 2 and 4—Knit 5, purl 3, and knit 5. Repeat purl 3 and knit 5 to the end of the row.

4. Row 3—Purl 5, knit 3, and purl 5. Repeat knit 3 and purl 5 to the end of the row.

5. Rows 6 and 8—Knit 1, purl 3, knit 5, and purl 3. Repeat knit 5 and purl 3 until the last stitch. Finish with knit 1.

6. Row 7—Purl 1, knit 3, purl 5, and knit 3. Repeat purl 5 and knit 3 until the last stitch. Finish with knit 1.

7. Repeat Steps 2 through 6 as desired.

Pyramid

1. Cast on 9 stitches at a minimum. Increase by multiple of 8 as needed.

2. Row 1—Purl 1, knit 7, and purl 1. Repeat knit 7 and purl 1 to the end of the row.

3. Row 2 and all even rows—Knit 1 and purl 1.

4. Row 3—Purl 2, knit 5, and purl 3. Repeat knit 5 and purl 3 to the last 7 stitches. Finish with knit 5 and purl 2.

5. Row 5—Purl 3, knit 3, and purl 5. Repeat knit 3 and purl 5 to the last 6 stitches. Finish with knit 3 and purl 3.

6. Row 7—Purl 4 and knit 1. Purl 7. Repeat knit 1 and purl 7 to the last 5 stitches. Finish with knit 1 and purl 4.

7. Row 9—Knit 4, purl 1, and knit 7. Repeat purl 1 and knit 7 to the last 5 stitches. Finish with purl 1 and knit 4.

8. Row 11—Knit 3, purl 3, and knit 5. Repeat purl 3 and knit 5 to the last 6 stitches. Finish with purl 3 and knit 3.

9. Row 13—Knit 2, purl 5, and knit 3. Repeat purl 5 and knit 3 to the last 7 stitches. Finish with purl 5 and knit 2.

10. Row 15—Knit 1, purl 7, and knit 1. Repeat purl 7 and knit 1 to the end of the row.

11. Row 16—Knit 1 and purl 1.

12. Repeat Steps 2 through 10 again, as desired.

Waning Moon Shawl

Supplies:

Needles—US 5 or 3.75 mm

Yarn—fingering weight, 200 yards

Extra—blocking pins

Gauge and Size—

Gauge—19 S X 36 R in 4 inches, textured pattern after blocking

Size—70-inch long x 13 inches at longest point

Instructions:

1. Longtail cast on 12 stitches.

2. Knit 2 rows.

3. Knit the waning moon pattern:

   a) Row 1—On the right side, knit 1, yarn over, and repeat 2 times. Knit to the front and back of the stitch and then knit to the last 3 stitches. Knit to the stitch's front and back, yarn over, and knit 1, repeating yarn over and knit 1 again.

   b) Row 2—On the wrong side, knit 3, purl to the last 3 stitches, and knit 3.

   c) Row 3—Knit 1, yarn over, and repeat 2 times. Knit to the front and back of the stitch, then purl 1, and knit 1. Purl 2 and knit 2, repeating this pattern to the last 4 stitches. Purl 1, knit to the front and back of the stitch, yarn over, and knit 1, repeating yarn over and knit 1 again.

d) Row 4—Knit 4 and purl 1. Repeat knit 2 and purl 1 until the last 4 stitches. Finish with knit 4.

e) Row 5—Knit 1, yarn over, and repeat 2 times. Knit to the front and back of the stitch, purl 1, yarn over, slip, slip, knit, knit 2 together, and yarn over. Purl 2, yarn over, slip, slip, knit, knit 2 together, and yarn over, repeating this pattern to the last 4 stitches. Purl 1, knit to the front and back of the stitch, repeat yarn over, and knit 1 two times.

f) Row 6—Knit across the row.

g) Row 7—Repeat Row 1.

h) Row 8—Repeat Row 2.

i) Row 9—Repeat Row 3.

j) Row 10—Repeat Row 4.

k) Row 11—Knit 1, yarn over, and repeat 2 times. Knit to the front and back of the stitch. Knit 2 together, yarn over, purl 2, yarn over, slip, slip, and knit, repeating this pattern to the last 3 stitches. Knit to the front and back of the stitch. Finish with yarn over and knit 1 repeating 2 times.

l) Row 12—Knit across the row.

4. Repeat Step 3 at least 9 times or until the shawl is your desired length.

5. Create the border:

a) Repeat Rows 1 and 2 of the Waning Moon patterns.

b) Row 3—Knit 3, purl to the front and back of the stitch, and knit 1. Purl to the front and back of the stitch 2 times and then knit 1. Repeat purl to the front and back of the stitch two times and then knit 1 until the last 4 stitches. Finish by purling to the front and back of the stitch and then knit 3.

c) Row 4—Knit 5 and purl 1. Knit 4, purl 1, and repeat this pattern until the last 5 stitches. Finish with knit 5.

d) Row 5—Knit 2, purl 2, and knit 1. Purl 4, knit 1, and repeat this pattern until the last 5 stitches. Finish with purl 2 and knit 3.

e) Row 6—Repeat Row 4.

f) Row 7—Knit across the row.

g) Row 8—Knit 3, purl to the last 3 stitches, and knit 3.

h) Row 9—Knit across the row.

i) Row 10—On the wrong side, bind off knit wise.

Chapter 9: Fixing the Common Mistakes in Knitting

You know that, no man is free from mistake. Doing mistake is a habit of human. The man who do not mistake is either a devil or an angel. Whatever the level of a knitter, he/ she is prone to do mistake. The expert knitters may also make mistakes very often. So, mistakes may happen with you too. But you will be glad to know that, it's not a great problem if you know what mistakes may occur and their possible solutions. With this I am going to tell you about the probable and most common mistakes of knitting so that, you can find them easily. I am also going to discuss about the step by step easy solutions of those mistakes. Please keep your eyes fixed here.

1. **If you find a twisted stitch:**

In case of knit side: When you wrap the yarn incorrectly just the previous row this mistake may happen. Stitch dropping is also another cause of such type of mistakes.

In case of purl side: The backward or twisted purl stitch looks somewhat different from the regular purl stitch. For such case, the back loop of this stitch remains closer to the needle tip comparing the front loop. You can correct this type of mistake by purling it just over the back loop.

2. If you find dropped stitch:

In case of knit side: A dropped stitch is seen very often in knitting cloth. If you trace out such a problem, you need to work on exactly at the place where you have found the dropping stitch. If this thing occurs in the case of one row just, then you can fix it easily. For correcting this mistake, you need to place your right-hand needle just through the stitch which is dropped along with the loose stand which is horizontally situated just behind the particular dropped stitch. Then fix it using the left-hand needle.

In case of purl side: If you find a dropped purl stitch in a single row, then you may try to fix it in this method. For this you should work only the stitch which has dropped. At that time, you should ensure that the loose stand is laid just in front of the particular stitch which is dropped. Then, as like the knit stitch fixing method, you need to insert your right or working needle through the dropped stitch. Now you need to lift the stitch which is dropped with the help of your left needle. Now your duty is to transfer your newly created purl to the left-hand needle again. For doing this you need to place your left-hand needle through the stitch after slipping the right-hand needle from the stitch.

3. If you find a running stitch:

Do you know what the running stitch is? If you find more than one dropped stitch in more than a row, then you can consider it as running stitch. It is not so tough job to correct this mistake. If you want to fix the mistake you just need a crochet hook. Using the crochet hook with a very easy way you can fix the running stitch.

4. If you find incomplete stitches:

If there exists any stitch where the yarn has held the needle but really not inserted into the loop for pulling stitch, then it is called incomplete stitch. For correcting the incomplete stitch, you just need to work on the particular incomplete stitch. You need to place your right or working needle into the incomplete stitch which is held by the left-hand needle and move it back and forth for fixing the error.

5. If you find an extra stitch:

You can find an extra or an extra stitch just at the edge of your stitched cloth. In general, the first stitch has just one loop, but when you bring your yarn back just over your needle top, then instead of one loop, you find two loops which is the cause for generating the extra stitch mistake. If you want to avoid this type of mistake, you just need to be careful somewhat. You need to ensure that, the yarn is kept under the needle especially when you are taking it back for knitting the first stitch. Nothing is complex here. Just keep your yarn at the front side of your needle at the time of beginning the stitch. You need not to do anything more.

Chapter 10: Finishing Your Task

You know that things that, "All are well that ends well". The finishing steps of knitting are very vital as the beauty of your cloth depends much on smooth finishing. If you can't do a good finish all of your hard work will turn into failure as you will not a good-looking cloth. After doing all the things you need to tie up the loose ends of your stitch and make a combination of different color. You should keep up a color harmony when attaching the loose ends. A good finishing work may present you a gorgeous and outstanding cloth where a bad finishing may give you just a junk and mesh of clothes.

With this I am going to tell you all the things in a brief of finishing tasks. Finishing work mainly includes the following three things.

1. Ends weaving

2. Blocking

3. Seaming

Let's go somewhat deeper with these three things.

1. **Ends weaving:** Weaving is much important for joining your different color fabrics. Good weaving has no option to make a handsome finished product. In fact, weaving is done through the opposite end of knitted fabric. For accomplishing this work at first you need to untie the knot that you have made at the time of joining new yarn. Then make some free loops and work on it. Please check again and again just the right side of your fabric because you need to make sure that, there has no puckering at the place where the ends started.

2. **Blocking:** Blocking is another very important thing that you need to know if you want to do a good finishing as if you don't do good blocking your fabric will look just sloppy whatever your knitting quality is. Blocking is must for you to give appropriate shape to your knitted fabric.

Basically, there have two main types of blocking. The first one is wet blocking and the second one is steam blocking. It's up to you that which one you will select. It depends on your personality and the available equipment. Here I am going to discuss briefly the two kinds of blocking.

a) **Wet blocking system for you:** As the name shows in this blocking system you need to apply water on your knitted fabric. You can follow different ways to apply water on your fabric. Simply you can immerse your fabric in the bucket which is full of cool water. Then squeeze the cloth and stretch the fabric just as your determined or desired measurement on the board or on the floor. Then allow the cloth to dry completely. It may take 24 hours or more. Again, you may follow another system for applying water on your knitted fabric. You can pin the cloth first on a board at your desired measurement then spray water on the cloth until it becomes completely wet. But this method looks somewhat laborious than the immersing method. The rest things are as same as the immersing method. You could not use the cloth for further work until it dries completely.

b) **Steam blocking system for you:** If you want to block with steam you need some special equipment like hot steaming iron or handheld steamer. For blocking in this process at first you need to pin your fabric according to your desired measurement. Then use your handheld steamer or hot steam iron over the fabric. If you use the steam iron, please make sure that, the iron is not touching your fabric at the time of steaming. Once you will find your fabric completely damp, then stop steaming and allow your fabric to dry. The good factor is that, in case of steam blocking the clothes dry so quickly comparing the wet blocking system. It may take only 1-2 hours where the wet blocking generally takes 24 hours or more for complete drying of the cloth.

3. **Seaming:** You have completed everything. Now one more step to get a complete knitted product which you can wear. Do you know what the thing is? Now you just need to sew your knitted fabrics together. In knitting work this process is known as seaming. You just need a needle and yarn for accomplishing this work. You will find different methods for sewing the fabrics you have knitted. Using any one of the convenient techniques you can sew vertically and horizontally your knitted cloth parts. Now you are almost done my dear.

Chapter 11: FAQ

Why is knitting a good skill to have?

Knitting is a brilliantly useful skill that can help you create a wide variety of your own products – everything from toys to clothing. But, not only that, it's scientifically proven to improve your mood, mind and body. It's a therapeutic skill which you will not regret learning!

How do you read a knitting chart?

The best way to read a knitting chart is in detail in this guide, in the Knitting Charts.

What I need to buy to start off knitting?

The Supplies of this guide gives you the basics of what you need to start knitting. However, the yarns, needles and anything extra you'll need for a specific pattern will be listed as one of the first pieces of information.

How do you do double-pointed knitting?

Double pointed needles are generally used for knitting in the round on projects that are too small for circular needles. They are often purchased in sets of 5. Here is a brilliant guide for how to use them, with these main top tips:

- o Cast on to 1 double pointed needle.
- o Then slip ½ the stitches onto another needle.
- o Then a third onto another.
- o Use a fourth needle to knit.

Does it cost a lot to knit?

Knitting can be done very cheaply **if you know the right places to look**. Local haberdashery stores will sell a wide range of products from high quality to budget, so it really is a skill that applies to everyone.

What is an easy way to learn how to knit?

The step-by-step guides provided in the Stitches of this guide will get you started.

How do you knit with 3 needles?

You will often use 3 or more needles when working with double pointed needles.

What are the differences for English and continental methods for knitting?

Everyone has their own preference when it comes to knitting style. You will eventually develop your own.

- **English Knitting**
  - Hold yarn in right hand
  - Throw yarn when wrapping
  - Easier with chunky weight yarns
- **Continental Knitting**
  - Hold yarn in left hand
  - Pick the yarn when wrapping
  - Faster when you're knitting the knit stitch

- o Alternating stitches is easier

- o Easier for crochets to learn

What is knitting in tandem?

Tandem knitting is a technique for knitting socks or gloves or anything in the round that comes in pairs and uses 9 DPNs, it casts on for both items in the pair at the same time, and involves completing a portion of one of the pair, then the same portion of the other item of the pair.

Is it hard to knit a scarf?

In the Patterns of this guide, you will find a pattern for a knitted scarf designed specifically for beginners. Scarves can be made by anyone at any skill level. If you're an advanced knitter, your creations can be much more complex and embellished.

Is crocheting harder than knitting?

Crocheting **is a different skill to knitting** in the way that it uses one hook rather than two needles. Different people prefer different skills so practicing both is the best way to figure out which one you personally find easier and more suitable.

Where can I find some great knitting patterns?

Knitting patterns can be found in haberdashery stores, but they are also available in abundance online. Just type 'Knitting Patterns' into any search engine and you will be spoilt for choice.

What are the next steps once you've worked through this guide?

This book gives you all the basics you need for starting knitting. Once you have gotten to grips with all of the stitches and patterns provided, it is time to move on to more complex patterns – you can maybe even create your own! Once you have mastered this skill, the possibilities are endless.

Conclusion

When some people think about weaving, they visualize little old grannies gradually passing the hours away, yet not any longer. This publication, "Knitting for Beginners," animates and also enlightens readers that Knitting is a fantastic leisure activity that can offer anybody with a huge selection of enjoyment and relaxation - in addition to adorable blankets, headscarves, hats, apparel as well as more! You can discover how to produce handmade knits for yourself and also for other individuals, and you can do this with merely a little technique and also perseverance. When you give a lovingly knit present, component of you enters into it, which, in turn, produces one of a kind, unique treasure. Your time, ability, the vibrant shade of yarn you select, even the nostalgic thoughts and also sensations you have as you work all end up being a part of your beautiful weaved gift.

Below Are Some Advantages of Knitting:

Knitting Is Good for The Brain

The focus calls for complying with a pattern as well as keeping an eye on which yarn (and even which needles) we're utilizing, computing just how much yarn is required, building up stitches and also rows, plus learning new skills as we grasp new stitches and novel patterns. All these have been shown to avoid moderate cognitive disability, the decrease in the power of understanding: reasoning, thinking, and also memory.

An international research study involving over 3,000 knitters revealed that the more frequently individuals weaved, the far better their cognitive function.

And knitting benefits both sides of the brain: right for creativity, left for logic as well as mathematics.

Weaving Is Friendly

It can be if you integrate knitting with seeing friends. It is as if knitting is portable so that you can take it with you for five-o'clock tea, pints in the pub, or to waste time while traveling (out aircraft, though).

There are checkouts to yarn stores as well as crafting shows. Whether you go alone or with good friends, browsing yarn, package, or being inspiring by someone else's job can be an actual discussion starter.

And after that, there's virtual sociability using social media sites. Complying with specialist knitters and also developers, seeing buddies' newest operate in progression, and also revealing your own soon make you feel component of an online neighborhood.

Weaving Makes You Calm

The balanced, repeated actions of relocating the yarn as well as the needles and also the concentration required to do it appropriately silence the chatter in your mind and even the more you do it, the better you feel.

The international study that showed a web link between knitting and brainpower also revealed a significant connection between knitting regularity and sensation calmness.

According to the Benson-Henry Institute for Mind-Body Medicine at Massachusetts General Hospital, the repetition of the motions of knitting can elicit the 'relaxation action,' representing a lowering of breathing price, heart rate, and high blood pressure.

Knitting Is an Economic Pastime

Provided you'll locate some extortionately valued threads in your local haberdashery store (if you're fortunate enough to have one), yet not whatever requires is to be made from cashmere.

Weaving Can Be A Present

Aside from giving a person something you've weaved for them; you can likewise hand down your expertise.

Educating someone to knit face-to-face is the very best method to learn, and showing a buddy, kid, or grandchild how to knit is super fun and also sets them up with a fulfilling leisure activity permanently.

You can grab a sphere of yarn for a couple of extra pounds, and needles for less.

Knitting Widens Your Wardrobe

Not just can you make things to put on, yet you can tackle the function of the stylist because just how these garments (or house makes) turn out is under your control.

Like the cut yet not the color? Knit it in your favorite. And sometimes you do not require a pattern, like with a headscarf. Cast on, with whatever woolen you desire, and keep going up until your choice is complete.

Knitting Increases Your Self-Confidence

Understanding techniques, adhering to a pattern or directions, and completing a project, as well as making something that didn't exist before, should make you feel pleased with yourself.

CPSIA information can be obtained
at www.ICGtesting.com
Printed in the USA
BVHW091056220221
600778BV00007B/728